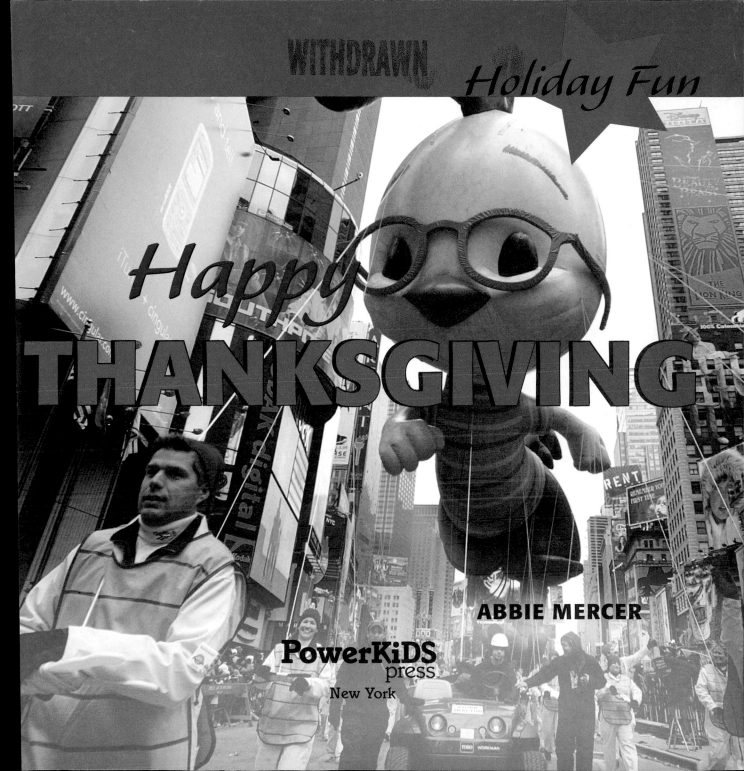

Happy THANKSGIVING

ABBIE MERCER

PowerKiDS press

New York

For Matt Tracey, even though Andes mints do not make an appearance

Published in 2008 by The Rosen Publishing Group, Inc.
29 East 21st Street, New York, NY 10010

First Edition

Editor: Amelie von Zumbusch
Book Design: Julio Gil
Photo Researcher: Nicole Pristash

Photo Credits: Cover, pp. 1, 7, 17, 19, 21 © Getty Images; p. 5 © www.istockphoto.com/Sean Locke; pp. 9, 13, 15 © Shutterstock.com; p. 11 © www.istockphoto.com/Yohan Juliardi.

Library of Congress Cataloging-in-Publication Data

Mercer, Abbie.
  Happy Thanksgiving / Abbie Mercer.
      p. cm. — (Holiday fun)
  Includes index.
  ISBN-13: 978-1-4042-3807-7 (library binding)
  ISBN-10: 1-4042-3807-7 (library binding)
  1. Thanksgiving Day—Juvenile literature. I. Title.
  GT4975.M466 2007
  394.2649—dc22
                                          2007000916

Manufactured in the United States of America

Contents

What Is Thanksgiving?

Thanksgiving is a holiday when people gather to eat a feast and enjoy one another's company. At first, Thanksgiving was a **harvest celebration**. People celebrated how thankful they were that they would have enough food to eat in the coming year. Today, people remember all the good things in their lives, such as food, homes, family, and friends, on Thanksgiving.

The date of Thanksgiving changes from year to year, but it always falls on the same day of the week. In the United States, the fourth Thursday in November is Thanksgiving. In Canada, Thanksgiving is the second Monday in October.

Thanksgiving is a time for family fun and feasting!

Thanksgiving is a holiday that brings people together. **Millions** of people travel by train, plane, or car to spend Thanksgiving with family or friends each year. In the United States, the day before Thanksgiving is one of the busiest days of the year to travel. Airports are always very crowded around Thanksgiving, since more than four and a half million people travel by plane on that weekend.

Many people spend Thanksgiving with their families. People who have small families or families who live far away often decide to celebrate with friends instead. Whom do you celebrate Thanksgiving with?

These travelers are waiting for trains at New York's Pennsylvania Station on the day before Thanksgiving.

Turkeys

Wherever you celebrate Thanksgiving, you will likely have a big feast. The chief dish at most people's Thanksgiving dinner is turkey. While most of the turkeys people eat were raised on farms, there are also wild turkeys. Wild turkeys live in North America. Both male wild turkeys and male turkeys on farms have folds of skin, called wattles, which hang over their necks. However, only wild turkeys are able to fly.

Every Thanksgiving, Americans eat more than 530 million pounds (240 million kg) of turkey! **Vegetarians** often eat **tofu** in the shape of a turkey for Thanksgiving.

Male turkeys are also called gobblers or tom turkeys. Tom turkeys can push their tail feathers up into a fan.

How to Make a Pinecone Turkey

Let's make a pinecone turkey in honor of Thanksgiving!

1 Start your pinecone turkey by finding a pinecone. The bits coming out of a pinecone are called scales.

2 Look carefully at the picture on page 11. Draw a head for the turkey. Make sure to add a bill and an eye. Color in the turkey's head.

3 Draw a fan shape. This will be the turkey's tail. Draw in the shapes of the feathers. Color in the tail.

4 Cut out the head and the tail. Slide the head into the scales at the flat end of the cone. Slide the tail between the scales at the cone's tip. Your turkey should look like the one on page 11.

More Thanksgiving Foods

Turkey is just one of the many foods people eat at Thanksgiving. Lots of Thanksgiving foods are closely tied to turkey. For example, stuffing is a mix of bread, vegetables, and seasonings that is cooked inside the turkey. The juices that run out of the turkey are used to make a topping called gravy that is poured over turkey. People also put a topping called cranberry sauce on turkey. Cranberries are red berries with a sharp taste.

Many people end their Thanksgiving feast with pumpkin pie. People also eat pies made with apples or nuts called pecans.

Vegetables, like potatoes, sweet potatoes, and green beans, are part of most people's Thanksgiving feasts.

How to Make a Pumpkin Pie

Pumpkin pie tastes great and is not too hard to make. Make sure to ask an adult to help you use the oven, though.

1 Set the oven to 425° F (218° C). Break three eggs into a bowl and beat, or quickly mix, them. Mix ½ cup sugar, ½ teaspoon cinnamon, ½ teaspoon cloves, ½ teaspoon nutmeg, ½ teaspoon ginger into the eggs.

2 Add a 15-ounce (425 g) can of pureed, or squashed, pumpkin to the mixture from step 1. Then add ½ cup (180 ml) cream. Mix it all together well.

3 Pour the mixture into a piecrust like the girl on page 15. You can buy a premade piecrust, or you can make your own piecrust.

4 Put the pie in the oven and bake it for about 45 minutes. Take the pie out and let it cool for an hour before eating it.

Thanksgiving Traditions

Eating a big meal is just one of many Thanksgiving **traditions**. Watching football games on TV is a big part of many Americans' Thanksgiving Day. There are always two football games on TV on Thanksgiving. A football team called the Detroit Lions plays in one of the games. The Dallas Cowboys play in the other.

Parades are another Thanksgiving tradition. Many cities and towns hold Thanksgiving parades. The largest Thanksgiving parade is the Macy's Thanksgiving Day Parade. It is held every year in New York City. The parade has marching bands, well-known singers, **floats**, and giant balloons.

This Chicken Little balloon from the Macy's Thanksgiving Day Parade is more than 60 feet (18 m) tall!

Thanksgiving traditions have built up over time, but the holiday dates back to 1621. In the fall of 1621, a group of English settlers held a feast with a group of **Wampanoag** Native Americans in Plymouth, Massachusetts. This feast is often called the first Thanksgiving.

The English settlers had arrived in Massachusetts in November 1620. The winter that followed was cold. The settlers did not have enough food. Many settlers died during the winter. The following year, Wampanoags showed the settlers how to find and grow food. That fall, the settlers had a good harvest and celebrated with a feast.

Today, people show how the Wampanoags and settlers lived at this living history museum in Massachusetts.

The First Thanksgiving

Though the English settlers and Wampanoags had a feast, it was different from a modern Thanksgiving meal. For one thing, their harvest celebration lasted three days! There were more than 100 people at the feast. The settlers' houses were small, so they set up tables and ate in the street.

No one knows if they ate turkey at the feast. We do know that the settlers and Wampanoags ate fish, duck, and venison, or deer meat. They also ate vegetables, like corn, onions, and squash. They ate most of the food with their hands, because did not have forks.

This woman is showing how the English settlers prepared their food. They had no stoves, so they cooked over fires.

The Spirit of Thanksgiving

Thanksgiving traditions have changed a lot since its beginning hundreds of years ago. However, people still use this holiday to think about all the good things in their lives.

Many people also think about those who have been less **fortunate** than them. They collect food to give to people who do not have enough to eat. Some people work in a soup kitchen on Thanksgiving. Soup kitchens are places where poor people can get a free meal. This is just one way to honor this holiday. How do you celebrate Thanksgiving?

Glossary

celebration (seh-luh-BRAY-shun) Things done to honor a special time.

floats (FLOHTS) Low, flat trucks that carry people and sets in a parade.

fortunate (FORCH-net) Lucky.

harvest (HAR-vist) A season's gathered crop.

male (MAYL) Having to do with men or boys.

millions (MIL-yunz) A very large number.

parades (puh-RAYDZ) Marches in honor of an important person or day.

tofu (TOH-foo) A soft, white food made from vegetables called soybeans.

traditions (truh-DIH-shunz) Ways of doing something that have been passed down over time.

vegetarians (veh-juh-TER-ee-unz) People who do not eat meat.

Wampanoag (wom-puh-NOH-ag) A group of Native Americans who live in Massachusetts and Rhode Island.

Index

Web Sites

Due to the changing nature of Internet links, PowerKids Press has developed an online list of Web sites related to the subject of this book. This site is updated regularly. Please use this link to access the list: www.powerkidslinks.com/hfun/thanks/